I0845660

Revolution of Robotics

Today's Innovations Shaping Our Tomorrow

Table of Contents

Chapter 1. Introduction

In an era where technology dominates every facet of our lives, the "Revolution of Robotics: Today's Innovations Shaping Our Tomorrow" takes you on an awe-inspiring journey through the rapidly evolving landscape of robotics. This Special Report unpacks the intricacies of this high-tech field in a comprehensible, down-to-earth manner, removing the intimidating layer of technical jargon. From our daily chores to high-level operations, robotics is making inroads into our reality in ways unimagined a decade ago. If you've ever wondered about the future shared with automated machines, this groundbreaking dossier is a must-read. It takes you by the hand and leads you to a tomorrow where your imagination is the only limit. Engage with the insights on these pages, and you'll find yourself investing not only in a document, but in a future molded by the power and potential of robotics.

Chapter 2. Dawn of the Robotic Age: Historical Context

Throughout recorded history, automation has been a harbinger of progress, improving efficiency in labor-intensive sectors. As we trace this evolution, it's necessary to go back centuries, not merely decades, to understand the fundamental idea that gave birth to what we now call robotics.

Our journey starts with the Greeks in ancient Alexandria - a city, which once stood as the epitome of knowledge and innovation. It was here that inventors like Hero of Alexandria developed devices that could operate without human intervention.

Hero devised what is understood to be the earliest known programmable machine - an automated theater powered by a binary-like system of ropes, knots, and simple machines able to perform a play lasting ten minutes. These machines were not robotics in modern understanding but rather mechanized tools that showcased the salient concept of automation.

Fast forward a millennium or so, works of al-Jazari, the 12th-century Muslim inventor from Medieval Iraq, also exhibited the rudimentary shape of automation. Among his numerous inventions, the musical automata and water-powered humanoid servants stand out as ancestors of today's robotics. The impact of these innovations would reverberate through the ages, shaping what we now know as the discipline of robotics and automation.

2.1. Emergence of Modern Robotics

Jumping from the philosophical and mechanical groundwork laid by these ancient civilizations, the trajectory of automation took a major leap in the 18th and 19th centuries.

The Industrial Revolution during this period instigated further development of mechanized tools. The advancement in steam power, hydrodynamics, and later electrification led to the birth of some astounding automated machines, which in essence were a tangible form of the philosophies embedded in ancient systems.

There was Jacques de Vaucanson's Digesting Duck in the 18th century, which mimicked a duck eating, digesting, and releasing waste. The comprehensive system of gears, cams, and cranks inside the duck represented a closed-loop system, a primary feature of modern robotics.

In the 19th century, Charles Babbage developed the "Difference Engine," a mechanical device to compute mathematical problems. While this notion of mechanical computing began to emerge, Ada Lovelace recognized the true potential of the device and described the concept of an all-purpose machine. Lovelace is often credited with the first algorithm intended for implementation on Babbage's Analytical Engine, making her the first programmer in history.

2.2. 20th Century to Present: The True Dawn of Robotics

The 20th century marked the dawn of actual robotics as we recognize it today. American inventor George Devol registered the first robot patent in 1954 for Universal Automatic Device (Unimate), an industrial robot. The Unimate was later installed in a general motors plant in 1961, undertaking hot and potentially hazardous tasks of die casting.

Around the same time, Joseph Engelberger, often referred to as the "Father of Robotics," recognized the potential of these programmed devices. This led to the creation of the first robotics company, Unimation.

The late 20th century saw tremendous upheaval and exploration in the field of robotics. In 1970, Stanford's Victor Scheinman invented the Stanford Arm, the revolutionary design that is the basis for the robot arm design still extensively used in industries today. Further, the late 20th century saw the advancement in AI (Artificial Intelligence), which ushered in the era of autonomous robots – robots that can perform tasks without human intervention.

21st-century robotics were dramatically influenced by advancements in sensing and AI. With sophisticated sensors, robots can interpret and maneuver in their surroundings better than ever before. Advancements in AI have enabled robots to make decisions, learn from their experiences, and even collaborate with humans, marking the beginning of cobotics (collaborative robots).

In the 21st century, robots have swiftly moved from factory floors to homes, hospitals, farms, and even to the realms of space. The Mars Rover expeditions, autonomous cars, robotic surgery systems, drones, and household robots represent this shift. The integration of cloud technology, big data and IoT, improved robotics' efficiency, transforming it from a specialized sector to a pervasive part of modern life, thus marking the dawn of the truly robotic age.

In retracing the history of robotics, it's clear that from the simple automated devices of ancient civilizations, through the Industrial Revolution cogwork automatons to the electronic and AI-infused designs of modern times, robotics has evolved to become an integral part of our lives. This narrative illustrates that as long as there is human curiosity and a passion for innovation, there will be new robotic forms to change the way we live, work, and interact with the world.

As we continue to advance in robotics, it isn't just hardware and technology shaping the direction, but a combination of ethical norms, regulations, visionary entrepreneurial spirit, and societal acceptance that will guide us through the next stages of the robotics revolution. The dawn of the robotic age is not only a testament to human creativity and foresight but a beacon guiding us to a future where robotics, automation, and artificial intelligence become a ubiquitous part of our daily lives. The dawn is here, and the day promises much excitement.

Chapter 3. Understanding Robotics: Fundamental Principles

In recent times, robotics has emerged from the realms of science fiction and is fast becoming part of our everyday lives. A whole new era is upon us as robots begin to infiltrate various sectors, ranging from manufacturing to health care, and from domestic services to entertainment. A comprehensive understanding of robotics, however, requires appreciation of the principles upon which this technology is based.

Chapter 4. Robots and Robotics: Demystifying the Jargon

In simplest terms, a robot is a machine capable of carrying out complex series of actions automatically, particularly those programmable by a computer. This definition, while simple, paves way for discrepancies due to the broad range of machines that can be classified as robots.

Robots can range from a simple automatic soap dispenser to a complex assembly line arm used in car manufacturing, all the way to sophisticated machines that can simulate human thought process and exhibit learning abilities. The key commonality across these varied examples is automation - an ability to operate or execute tasks independently, often relying on a form of programmatic control.

Robotics, on the other hand, is the interdisciplinary branch of engineering and science that includes mechanical engineering, electrical engineering, computer science, and others. It deals with the design, construction, operation, and use of robots, as well as computer systems for their control, sensory feedback, and data processing.

4.1. Basic Types of Robots

There are several ways to categorize robots; however, on the fundamental level, there are three basic types – stationary robots, wheeled robots, and humanoid robots.

- Stationary Robots: These are robots that perform their operations without movement. They can be found in industries manufacturing cars, electronic devices, and even in the medical sector for performing intricate surgeries.

- Wheeled Robots: This type of robots is mobile and often makes use of wheels to move around. Roomba, a robot that cleans floors is a popular example of this class.
- Humanoid Robots: These are robots that are designed to mimic the human form. Some, like Honda's Asimo, demonstrate incredible sophistication, capable of walking and running on uneven surfaces as well as interacting with the environment in semi-autonomous ways.

4.2. Assembling a Robot

Creating a robot can be thought of as a three-step process – designing, constructing, and programming.

Design involves creating the initial blueprint of the robot with the desired structure and functionality in mind. This often takes into consideration factors like the robot's final purpose, cost and complexity of development, and the intended environment of operation.

Construction ensues the design phase. This involves the choice of materials, which can range from simple cardboard to sophisticated metal alloys, and the assembly of electronic components such as motors, sensors, and control boards.

Finally, programming the robot entails inputting instructions into the machine to perform specific tasks. At a basic level, this could mean a pre-determined series of tasks executed regardless of external factors. More complex robots incorporate sensors and algorithms that enable them to react to their environment and make decisions based on the data they collect.

4.3. Anatomy of a Robot: Key Components

Every robot comprises of several key components, including a power supply, a control system (often a computer), actuation systems (like motors), sensors, end effectors (like a robotic hand or a tool), and a manipulator (like a robotic arm).

- Power Supply: Depending on the robot's design and intended use, the power may come from batteries, solar power, hydraulic or pneumatic power, or a tethered connection to an external power source.

- Control System: This is usually a computer or microcontroller that directs the actions of the machine.

- Actuation System: Motors are always present in some form, whether they drive the wheels of a mobile robot, the joints of a robotic arm, or the pistons of a hydraulic system.

- Sensors and Effectors: These components allow robots to interact with their environments. Sensors collect information that a robot's control system can use to make decisions, while effectors do the work that the robot is designed to do.

- Manipulator: An appendage or series of jointed segments usually connected to an end effector which enables the robot to perform its tasks.

4.4. The Robotics Process – Sense, Plan, Act

A simple yet powerful model to understand how a robot works involves a three-step process: sense, plan, act.

In the sensing phase, a robot uses sensory input to collect data about its environment. This information may come from any of a wide array of sensors, such as cameras, distance sensors, or temperature sensors, among others.

Planning involves processing the sensory data to make decisions. This might be a simple if-then rule ("if the sensor detects an obstacle, turn right"), or a complex set of algorithms that includes mapping, path planning, and object recognition.

Acting is the execution of these decided-upon tasks. In a complex robot, the acting phase is continually fed with the sensing and planning steps, providing for real-time, sensible action based on a continuously updated understanding of the environment.

4.5. The Future of Robotics

The field of robotics is on a path of rapid evolution, promising to profoundly impact our world. As advancements continue in machine learning, AI, sensor technologies, and material science, the capacities and applicability of robotics will only continue to grow.

A clear understanding of the fundamental principles of robotics aids in envisioning a future context where robots take on increasingly critical roles. These roles, while ever-evolving, remain rooted in the principles presented here: an amalgamation of robotic hardware and software to deliver specific tasks, where sensing, planning, and acting remain the prime functions, even as they become imbued with growing intelligence and flexibility.

And so, Robotics offers not just a glimpse, but an immersive journey into our upcoming reality – a reality where automated machines extend human capacities and redefine notions of progress. After all, the journey of understanding robotics is no less than capturing a foretaste of the future. It's the dawn of a new era, where the line between science fiction and reality fades away, making room for a chapter of human ingenuity that would reshape our world for years to come.

Chapter 5. Navigating the Language of Robotics: Terms and Definitions

As we embark on this journey through the realm of robotics, it's essential to familiarize ourselves with the language used. Having a clear understanding of the following terms and definitions will enhance comprehension and facilitate ease of navigation through this high-tech territory.

5.1. Terminology Related to Robots

Robot: A programmable, multifunctional manipulator designed to move material, parts, or specialized devices through variable programmed motions for a variety of tasks. Notably, they are designed to perform tasks without human intervention and can operate in environments unsuitable or hazardous for humans.

Humanoid Robot: Rooted in the term "humanoid" (resembling a human being), these robots have bodies built to mimic human form and function. They often possess limbs, a head, and a torso, and are used in research, public services, or labor tasks.

Biobot: Think biology meeting robotics. Biobots are a type of robot that mimics the behavior and functions of humans or animals. They are studied in the field of bio-robotics, which is interdisciplinary by nature.

Cobot : A portmanteau of 'collaborative' and 'robot,' cobots are robots intended to operate in conjunction with humans in a shared workspace. They often include safety features allowing for safe human interaction.

5.2. Key Control Systems

Actuator: A component of a machine responsible for moving or controlling a mechanism or system. In robotics, an actuator converts energy into physical motion intended to mimic the natural movements of a human or animal.

Servo: This is a type of actuator that provides a high level of control over position, velocity or acceleration. Servos are often seen in systems where swift and precise movements are critical, like a robotic arm.

Control System: A control system manages, commands, directs, or regulates the behavior of other devices or systems to achieve desired outputs. It engages with the environment, takes measurements, compares them to a standard, and then initiates corrective action, if needed.

5.3. Robotics Engineering Terms

Degrees of Freedom: This term refers to the independent physical movements that a robot arm can make. The more degrees of freedom, the more flexible a robot's movement can be. For example, human arms have seven degrees of freedom.

End Effector: The end effector is the part of the robot that interacts with the environment. In layman's terms, it serves as the robot's 'hand.' The nature of the end effector depends on its purpose — it could be a welding torch, camera, gripper, or even a paint spray.

Payload: In robotics, payload refers to the weight a robotic arm or system can lift and move. This determination is crucial for selecting the right robot for a job. Too light of a payload might mean inefficiency, while too heavy may cause system failure or safety risks.

5.4. Robotics Software and Algorithms

Simultaneous Localization and Mapping (SLAM): A key problem in robotics precisely involves knowing where a robot is and where it has been, which is central to SLAM. It involves a robot creating or updating a map of an unknown environment while keeping track of its location within this environment.

Path Planning: It is a critical concept in robotics relating to the problem of negotiating the best path from point A to B. Efficient path planning not just ensures a robot's function but can preserve battery life and increase longevity.

5.5. Troubleshooting Terms

Null Position: It refers to the origin or zero position for the robot. It's the base reference point from which all other positions or movements are calculated.

Robot Downtime: This is the period during which a robot is non-operational due to a malfunction or planned maintenance. Minimizing downtime is a key objective to maintain productivity.

In effect, these terms provide handles to navigate the technical discourse surrounding robotics. The sheer diversity seen in these terminologies reflects the vastness and complexity of this field. Nevertheless, even this complex language becomes intelligible and manageable once we devote time to learn it.

Only through comprehending these concepts can one uncover the fascinating interplay between robots and our world. As daunting as it may seem, rest assured, decoding this intricate language of automation is not beyond anyone's reach.

Chapter 6. The Everyday Robots: Robotics in Daily Life

As the sun peeks over the horizon, beeping gently replaces the trill of morning birds. It's not an alarm clock, but a robotic assistant, nudging its owner awake with a gentle and persistent reminder. Whether it's brewing your first cup of coffee, dusting off the dining table, or even assisting with personal healthcare, robots are steadily reshaping our everyday lives. These helpers are not just for the tech-savvy or the coders, though. They are quickly becoming as common as smartphones and personal computers once were.

6.1. Rise of Domestic Robots

Scratch beneath surface-level assumptions about the limited role of robots, and you'll find a plethora of uses. Domestic robots, for example, have moved beyond just vacuuming floors. Consider robotic lawn mowers like the Automower by Husqvarna, which tirelessly keeps your lawn neat while you spend your time elsewhere. Robotic devices also help with menial tasks like dusting, window cleaning, and even pet care. For instance, the Litter-Robot device automatically cleans and refills cat litter boxes, making pet maintenance more manageable.

Recent advancements in robotic technology have led to the invention of robots that can cook, too. The Moley Robotic Kitchen, set to be commercially available soon, is equipped with a pair of sophisticated robotic arms that emulate human movements. From pan-frying to stirring, these multifunctional robotic arms can execute a multitude of culinary tasks auto-driven by recipe instructions.

Beyond tasks within the home, robotic mail delivery and robotic garbage collection are also on the rise. As we make strides in automation technology, we inch closer to a day where we can conserve human labor for more complex tasks, while our robotic counterparts handle the monotony.

6.2. Robotics in Healthcare

Robotics are no longer just about completing physical tasks — they're making significant strides in healthcare too. From nurse robots like the Moxi robot, designed to assist with routine tasks in hospitals, to the da Vinci Surgical System which enables surgeons to perform delicate procedures with meticulous precision, robotics in healthcare are saving lives and optimizing patient care.

Remote assistance robots enable patients and doctors to communicate effectively even at a distance. The InTouch Vita robot, for instance, allows for real-time video consultations, facilitating the process of diagnosis and treatment. For elderly care, socially assistive robots like ElliQ aim to mitigate feelings of loneliness and isolation by providing companionship and mental stimulation.

Moreover, wearable robotics, such as bionic limbs and exoskeleton suits, are transforming the lives of individuals with physical disabilities. By restoring mobility, these devices are empowering those who use them to regain control over their lives, from everyday tasks to more complex activities.

6.3. Robotics in Education

Robotics is also extending its roots into education, offering unique opportunities for learning. LEGO's Mindstorms series, for instance, are kits that allow students to build their own robots and program them. This approach not only fosters computational thinking but also encourages problem-solving skills and creativity.

Online learning, accelerated by global events such as the coronavirus pandemic, is also leveraging advancements in robotics. Tutor robots, such as EMYS from Flash Robotics, provide a unique platform for interactive learning. These robots are capable of recognizing and displaying emotions, making the learning experience more engaging for students.

In the realm of higher education, universities are using robots to facilitate administrative tasks. These bots assist with tasks ranging from career guidance to handling queries about college policies and procedures, freeing up staff to focus on tasks requiring human finesse.

6.4. The Future of Everyday Robotics

It's clear we are only at the beginning of the robotics evolution. The future promises a multitude of advancements; personal drone assistants, robotic chefs, driverless cars, and even robots for personal grooming like hair-cuts are not so far ahead.

While these innovations are impressive, they come with their own challenges. Questions regarding job replacement, data privacy, ethical implications, and the widely feared 'robot uprising' need to be addressed as we move towards a future intertwined with robotics.

The road to tomorrow is paved with robots, and understanding their role in our daily life is the first step to harnessing their potential. These machines, once seen as mere figments of science fiction, are now tangible components of our reality, making our day-to-day life simpler and freeing us to focus on more nuanced tasks. It's a fascinating time — an era where technology and imagination meld together seamlessly, promising a future where the boundaries of what's possible are consistently being redefined.

Today, the button-press convenience of automation is already a reality, but tomorrow, we might just wake up to a world where robots are an extension of the self, an integral part of the human experience. It's an awe-inspiring thought, a glimpse into a future guided by robotics, but always powered by human ingenuity. As this new era dawns, we get to decide how we'll interact with our automated counterparts — not with fear, but with curiosity and a keen sense of anticipation.

Chapter 7. The Helpers in White Coats: Medical Robotics

From those quaint health centers in rural pockets to the immaculate halls of urban healthcare facilities, a revolution is steadily unfolding – softly imparted by tireless entities known as medical robots. These sophisticated machines, our helpers in white coats, are increasingly taking center stage, offering unprecedented opportunities to revolutionize healthcare, augment precision and reduce human error.

==Recent Advances in Medical Robotics==

The field of medical robotics has observed significant advancements over the years, making robotic systems an integral part of the modern healthcare landscape. A key development includes the Da Vinci Surgical System, which was the first FDA approved robotic surgical system. Da Vinici performs minimally invasive procedures with increased precision, reducing surgery time and patient recovery periods.

The Rosa Spine, another major landmark, allows neurosurgeons to precisely navigate the spine, improving the outcomes of complex spinal surgeries. Automated imaging systems like the CyberKnife provide non-invasive, targeted cancer treatments through a compact linear accelerator – a big leap forward in radiation therapy.

==Critical Role in Minimally Invasive Procedures==

The application of robotics in minimally invasive surgery (MIS) represents a significant stride in the medical field. These surgeries result in smaller incisions, less pain, and quicker recovery times compared to traditional surgery techniques.

Robotic-assisted surgeries, such as the da Vinci System, have immensely improved the accuracy of MIS. The robot enables surgeons to perform complex procedures through small incisions with the use of robotically-controlled instruments, thus enhancing precision and reducing the risk of complications.

==Exploring Nanorobotics in Healthcare==

Medical nanorobotics is a fast-evolving subfield of nanotechnology, promising transformative health solutions at molecular scales. Nanorobots, tiny bots no bigger than a blood cell, could deliver drugs directly to diseased cells, scrub arterial plaque, or perform cellular surgery. While still largely in the research phase, nanorobotics holds a remarkable potential to revolutionize treatments for various diseases, including cancer.

==The Reality of Robotic Prosthesis==

The scope of medical robotics extends to the domain of neuroprosthetics – a discipline that merges neurology with prosthetics. Advanced robotics technology has led to the development of next-generation prosthetics, imbued with the power of machine learning and biofeedback, which accurately mimics natural limbs.

Sophisticated robotic prostheses, such as the LUKE Arm, can perform diverse functions like gripping, pointing, and providing sensory feedback, thus restoring independence for thousands of amputees.

==Robotic System in Rehabilitation==

Medical robots have made a significant impact in patient rehabilitation, with machines like robot-assisted gait training devices aiding in the recovery of individuals with stroke and spinal cord injuries. Rehabilitation robots can assist in the intensive, repetitive movement therapy required by these patients, improving motor function and accelerating recovery times.

==Pharmacy Automation Systems==

From pill dispensing to sorting and labeling, pharmacy robotic systems are simplifying pharmacists' roles while increasing efficiency and reducing errors. The autonomous robots work by pre-programming the prescribed medicines, reminders, doses and route of administration, which significantly reduces the chances of medication errors, a global concern in healthcare delivery.

==Beyond The Horizon==

Remote operation of medical robots is a promising frontier, especially in areas with limited access to specialized doctors. Telepresence robots, for example, allow healthcare practitioners to interact with and examine patients from afar. Similarly, remote robotic surgeries – where surgeons operate from miles away – has made quality healthcare more accessible.

Medical robotics is paving its way into unchartered territories, offering promising frontiers for health and well-being. However, it's crucial to tread forward with cautious enthusiasm, for while the benefits are plenty, so are the challenges. Questions surrounding cost, ethics, reliability, and the ever-looming risk of technology dependence may impose some restraints on the pace of adoption.

Yet, amid uncertainties, one thing shines clear - medical robots, our helpers in white coats, have the potential to redefine healthcare. By redirecting tasks to precision-operating machines, healthcare professionals can shift their focus to the humanistic aspects of medical provision, leading to meaningful patient engagement and improved outcomes. Undeniably, the future of healthcare is here, propelled by the diligent revolution of medical robotics.

Chapter 8. Artificial Companions: The Rise of Social Robotics

One of the most profound aspects of contemporary robotic development lies in the realm of social robotics, where machines are not merely workers but also companions. Allowing for an interactive relationship with humans, these robotic companions offer a unique blend of machine efficiency with a quasi-human connection, transforming our perceptions about the possibilities of AI.

8.1. The Birth of Social Robotics

The inception of social robotics takes us back to the end of the 20th century. Computer scientists, innovators, and psychologists recognized the potential for robots to do more than just perform manual tasks; they could also interact socially with humans. Beginning with simple machines that could respond to basic voice commands, social robotics has blossomed into a field supporting highly intelligent machines capable of understanding and responding to human emotions, intentions, and needs.

8.2. A Leap in Human-Robot Relations

Social robots represent a significant leap forward in human-machine relations. Traditional robotics served primarily as tools, performing tasks in a multitude of sectors, including manufacturing and healthcare. However, their interaction with humans remained essentially one-way: humans issued commands; robots executed.

The introduction of social robotics shifted this dynamic. Advanced algorithms allow these robots to recognize and interpret human emotions, broadening the scope of their utility. This two-way interaction revolutionizes our understanding of what robots can do. We can communicate with them to alleviate loneliness, provide emotional support, learn, or simply enjoy a game.

8.3. Understanding Social Robots

Social robots are complex pieces of machinery, but their essence is straightforward. They are designed to interact socially with humans. They do this by employing advanced software that enables them to interpret and respond to human behavior. These interactive behaviors are presented through various formats, from facial cues to gestures and vocal tonality - all aimed at facilitating a more natural, and enjoyable, human-robot interaction.

8.4. Challenges and Breakthroughs

As expected, the journey of social robotics has been paved with both challenges and breakthroughs. The principal hurdle continues to be 'uncanny valley,' a concept describing a discomfort or eeriness felt by humans when robots appear almost, but not exactly, like real human beings. As we strive to make robots more human-like, this psychological phenomenon becomes more prevalent and poses a significant obstacle to the widespread adoption of social robots.

On the flip side, there have been monumental achievements. Robots like Sophia, developed by Hanson Robotics, have pushed boundaries with their high-level interactions and emotional understanding. As technology advances, so too does the sophistication of these machines, bringing social robots closer to the ultimate goal: seamless interaction with humans.

8.5. The Impact on Society

Far from science fiction, social robots are increasingly a part of our daily lives. The integration of these machines in homes and businesses around the world is slowly changing how we live, work, and play. Robots are offering companionship to elderly individuals and providing children with innovative, interactive learning platforms.

In businesses, social robots are serving customers, providing entertainment, and facilitating new ways of working. While these applications are currently in their infancy, the future possibilities of integrating social robots into society are vast.

8.6. Looking Towards the Future

As we look towards the future, the possibilities are virtually limitless. Enhancements in speech recognition, emotional understanding, and autonomous thinking will enable social robots to offer environmental-sensitive companionship, sophisticated customer service, and interactive educational experiences.

However, as we become more accustomed to interacting with our artificial companions, important ethical and privacy questions arise. How do we ensure that this technology is used responsibly? How do we protect privacy when robots are designed to learn from our behavior? These questions, while daunting, must be carefully considered as we forge ahead into a future powered by social robotics.

In conclusion, the field of social robotics holds enormous potential – for companionship, productivity, efficiency and learning. As we stand on the brink of a technological revolution, it's fascinating to imagine a world where social robots become an integral part of our lives. Yet, we must tread this path cautiously, remembering that these robots, despite their human-like interactions, lack the genuine consciousness and empathy inherently human.

Chapter 9. Robots at Work: Industrial Automation and Its Impact

The expanse of industrial automation leverages the immense power of robotics, helping evolve the nature of human work and increasing the efficiency of the production process. Today, robots are undeniably an integral part of many industries, performing tedious, repetitive, and precise tasks with an accuracy that often surpasses human capability.

9.1. The Rise of Industrial Robots

In the early 1960s, the first industrial robot, Unimate, was launched. This whirling mechanical arm could weld, move parts, and conduct other tasks, which, although simple by today's standards, were groundbreaking in that era. From these humble beginnings, robotic technology rapidly advanced thanks to innovations in computing and machinery, driving down cost and overcoming engineering challenges.

Today's industrial robots are increasingly versatile and intelligent. They can do far more than just simple, repetitive tasks. They can also make decisions based on sophisticated analysis, thanks to improvements in artificial intelligence and machine learning, gathering data from sensors, interpreting it, and making informed decisions.

9.2. Industrial Robots in the Manufacturing Sector

The manufacturing sector has been the most impacted by the dawn of industrial robotics. With the capability to work non-stop without fatigue, robots have provided manufacturing industries with supercharged productivity around the clock. They reduce costs by minimizing waste, ensuring consistency in quality, and reducing the time required for production.

Robots have been deployed in automobile manufacturing, electronics assembly, food processing, and pharmaceutical production among others. In auto assembly plants, for example, robots handle everything from welding to painting, performing the tasks with a preciseness that ensures uniformity in every single unit of production.

In electronics assembly, minute and repetitive tasks such as circuit board soldering and chip placement are done with robotic precision, reducing errors and improving efficiency. The advent of nanotechnology has also opened new doors for robotics in the manufacturing segment. They can perform precise, microscopic assembly work that could never have been executed by human hands.

==='Robots in the Supply Chain'

Automation in supply chain and logistics has revolutionized how goods and products are stored, transported, and shipped. Automated guided vehicles (AGVs) and autonomous mobile robots (AMRs) have become commonplace in warehouses and distribution centers, working alongside humans to streamline operations.

In large warehouses, robotic systems are used to sort, stack, and retrieve items, reducing the time taken to process orders. They also optimize storage by stacking goods to maximum heights that would be unsafe or inefficient for humans. AGVs and AMRs can quickly move goods around, guided by sophisticated software that plots the fastest and safest routes, and equipped with sensors and cameras to avoid collisions.

9.3. The Safety Paradox

In the industrial setting, there has always been a safety paradox when it comes to robotics. On one side, robots are deployed to handle dangerous tasks, preventing human exposure to hazardous working conditions. On the other side, there are safety concerns associated with their use, such as mishaps due to malfunctioning of equipment or a lack of adequate safety features.

However, the robotic industry has worked relentlessly towards enhancing safety features, adhering strictly to regulatory standards, and cultivating a safety culture. Compliance with ISO standards, the use of advanced sensors, and equipping robots with AI make the robots halt or slow down when a human worker comes too close, are some of the measures taken to ensure safety.

9.4. The Impact of Industrial Robots on Employment

A significant concern regarding the expansion of automation and robotics is the displacement of human workers. It's an undeniable fact that robots have replaced some jobs, primarily those involving repetitive, dangerous or physically demanding work.

However, they have also led to the creation of new jobs. Maintenance of these machines, programming, system integration and analysis are few among many roles that didn't exist before the advent of robotics. Moreover, by taking up mundane tasks, robots allow human workers to focus on more complex and value-adding tasks that require creativity, problem-solving skills, and intricate decision-making prowess.

9.5. Outlook and Future Possibilities

It's clear that the role of industrial automation is entrenched in our societies and economies. As the price-performance ratio of robots continues to improve, it's likely we'll see increased deployment in industries that are yet to leverage their full potential.

Advanced machine learning algorithms coupled with improved sensor technology will potentially lead to robots that can understand their surroundings better, learn from experience, and make more complex decisions. That could usher in a new wave of more versatile robots capable of performing tasks that need a high level of adaptability, such as handling unpredictable items in a warehouse or assembling custom products.

In summary, the journey of robotics in industrial automation has been nothing short of transformative. While challenges exist, the potential benefits in productivity, efficiencies, and the creation of new opportunities are too substantial to ignore. By embracing this technology, we can aspire to create a future that's safer, more productive, and driven by remarkable inventions and innovations.

Chapter 10. The Unseen Force: Robotics in Defense and Security

In any conversation about modern defense and security, a ruling sentiment prevails: the ever-increasing role robotics is destined to play. With its roots embedded deeply within the military system, robotics has come a long way from being simply experimental to now being pivotal in the context of national, regional, and global security. The boundaries of what is possible are continuously being pushed due to research in robotics, illuminating newer ways in which this unseen force can revolutionize defense mechanisms.

10.1. Military Prowess Bolstered by Robotics

In the fight against threats, both within and outside the nation's borders, the defense sector is pioneering the adoption of robotics in a bid to enhance military prowess. In an environment where precision, endurance, and performative consistency are paramount, robots emerge as an ideal solution.

Unmanned Aerial Vehicles (UAVs), or drones, are arguably the most recognized instance of premium military hardware that have transformed the theatre of war. These advanced tools allow soldiers to observe, explore, and engage in surveillances virtually from any part of the world. UAVs are armed with robust cameras, sensors, and often weaponry to take on missions that could otherwise compromise human life. They not only carry out impeccably precise strikes but also contribute to minimizing civilian casualties.

The origins of UAVs can be traced back to simpler radio-controlled aircraft used in World War II, demonstrating an early aptitude for remote warfare. Their usage has come a long way since then. Today, drones like the MQ-9 Reaper and the RQ-4 Global Hawk can fly at high altitudes, cover long distances, and stay airborne for extended durations while providing real-time data to ground control.

Robotic systems aren't limited to the air, though. Unmanned Ground Vehicles (UGVs) are increasingly used for reconnaissance, disarmament of explosives, and occasionally direct combat. Taking over high-risk operations, UGVs ensure enhanced operational safety while also caring for a soldier's wellbeing on the battlefield.

Take the example of PackBot, a series of military robots that have been extensively used in Afghanistan and Iraq. These armored robots, controlled via a console and joystick, are traditionally deployed for tasks such as bomb disposal, reconnaissance, and surveillance. The PackBot's slew of sensors can create a 3D map of the environment, while its nimble manipulator arm can defuse a deadly explosive.

10.2. Robotics in Naval Security

Shifting our gaze from the land to the sea, advancements in robotics are shaping not only warfare but also intelligence and surveillance operations. Unmanned Underwater Vehicles (UUVs), like their aerial and ground counterparts, are taking on dangerous tasks such as detecting mines, surveillance, inspecting underwater pipelines, and more.

One classic example is 'Sea Wasp,' a highly agile, remotely operated underwater vehicle. This robot has been specially designed to identify and neutralize lethal underwater explosives. Its ability to function effectively in harsh seawater makes it a crucial asset to naval and marine forces globally.

Similarly, solar Unmanned Surface Vessels (USVs) also appear to be a game-changer. These vessels continuously harvest energy from the sun, enabling them to stay operational on naval missions for extended periods.

10.3. Automation: Redefining Logistical Support

While combat and surveillance operations draw an overwhelming majority of the limelight in military robotics, one significant behind-the-scenes application of automation in the defense sector is providing logistical support.

Automated supply chain tools are used in large quantities for ferrying supplies, while robotic systems are responsible for maintenance functionalities within army bases. From moving heavy loads to loading and unloading supplies, automation in logistical support enables forces to maintain operation readiness while reducing dependence on human labor for these processes.

A prime example of this trend is the K-MAX helicopter developed by Kaman Aerospace in partnership with Lockheed Martin. This drone copter has been designed specifically for transporting cargo in rough terrains and difficult weather conditions. Due to its automation, the K-MAX is able to operate 24/7, improving the logistics supply chain of the defense forces significantly.

10.4. Future Possibilities

The future of robotics in defense and security poised teems with revolutionary possibilities. Concepts like autonomous 'swarms' that mimic behaviors observed in nature could revolutionize warfare strategies and rescue operations. AI-powered self-healing robots may take over extensive repair work during combat, reducing downtime in critical battlefield scenarios.

With 3D-printing technology, it is now possible to print drones on demand at remote locations. Developments in this space should allow military units to print and deploy equipments based on real-time needs.

However, as military robotics continue to develop and advance, ethical, legal, and security concerns need to be meticulously addressed. The evolution and application of robots in warfare should be paired with a robust framework that ensures moral and strategic implementation.

Navigating through complex political, military, and human rights considerations, the revolution of robotics in defense and security will undoubtedly be a key part of our tomorrow. It's an exciting time for this dynamic, rapidly evolving sector. The impact of this unseen force is only set to become more pronounced and decisive in the near future. Full of potential, the horizon is vast and wide open.

Chapter 11. Looking Ahead: Future Prospects of Robotics

As we peer into the future, the potential of robotics seems nothing short of phenomenal. They stand not as a far-off possibility, but as a burgeoning reality. At the cusp of this transformation, we are allowed a glimpse of what could be a future dominated by these creations of human ingenuity.

11.1. The Rise of Sophisticated Machines

The advancements in developing sophisticated robot models, undergirded by Machine Learning and AI, signal the advent of an era where robots will have nuanced intelligence akin to humans. The introduction of multimodal perception systems, which integrate lidar, radar, cameras, and other sensors to facilitate a robot's sense and interaction with the world, is augmenting the transition. This technology indeed is pivotal in autonomous vehicle design, industrial automation, and household robots.

As the 'nature' of future robots expands, they would be capable to adapt to and learn from their environments. Experts predict we might witness robots that can improvise around obstacles to perform tasks, an outstanding leap from automation to true autonomy.

11.2. Autonomous Robots: From Drones to Vehicles

Driven by AI algorithms, there are already examples of autonomous functioning robotics in our world today. Drones, for instance, are no longer just recreational gadgets. They are currently employed in parts of industrial inspection, agriculture, supply-chain and delivery services, and more.

With autonomous vehicular technology, cars that can park themselves are just the tip of the iceberg. Automatic vehicles can gradually take over tasks of driving, reducing human error and improving overall road safety.

11.3. Humanoid Robots and their Prospects

Technological strides are inching closer to robots that can convincingly emulate human behavior. Companies are earnestly prototyping humanoid robots - which can interact with their environment and carry out tasks in a human-like manner. Armed with advanced sensors, cameras, and AI, these robots can recognize and respond to the world around them according to programmed scenarios. Straight out of a sci-fi flick, these robots are set to revolutionize tasks ranging from simple housework to complex medical procedures.

11.4. The Surge of Collaborative Robots

Collaborative robots, or 'cobots,' working seamlessly alongside humans in various industries, mark another leap. Cobots are excellent for tasks that require high levels of dexterity and precision, tasks generally known as repetitive or even dangerous for human workers. They can uplift productivity and reduce costs in industries such as manufacturing and healthcare.

11.5. Robotics in Outer Space

The field of space exploration is reaping the benefits of robotics. Rovers are exploring celestial bodies, satellites are maintaining our telecommunications infrastructure, and autonomous robots are servicing the International Space Station. The future shall see more advanced devices working under extreme conditions, far beyond human capabilities.

11.6. Robot Ethics and Regulations

While the advances are impressive, they call for serious thought on the ethical implications of a robot-immersed future. Issues such as job displacement, data privacy, and the creation of autonomous weapons are raising concerns. Subsequently, the need for regulations and guidelines governing robot usage is becoming urgent.

11.7. Addressing the Skill Gap

The robotics revolution will bring forth a seismic shift in the job market, rendering some jobs redundant while creating new roles. This calls for nations to address the imminent skill gap and invest resources in appropriate education and training programs.

This glimpse paints an exciting, yet challenging, picture of our future in robotics. Robots can not only augment our lives but also help solve some of the world's pressing issues. However, as we foray into this territory, it's vital to navigate the accompanying challenges with thoughtful planning and regulation. This is the dawn of the robotics era, where possibilities born from the human mind hold the key to shaping our future.

To conclude, we affirm that while we can't predict the future with certainty, the seeming inevitability of a world where robotics are integral to our daily lives is clear. In this world, innovation is a constant and our imagination, indeed, the only limit. The future of robotics lies within our hands; our actions today will shape the world our successors inherit tomorrow.

Chapter 12. Ethics, Regulations, and Robotics: Navigating the Uncertainties

In an age where the pace of technological advancement appears to accelerate exponentially, one of the most exciting yet contentious developments is undoubtedly the rise of robotics. As with any revolutionary technology, robotics presents a multitude of ethical and regulatory challenges alongside its myriad opportunities and benefits.

Technology often outstrips legislation, rapidly advancing ahead of societal norms and legal frameworks which are slow to adapt to new concepts and technologies. As robotics penetrates every aspect of daily life, staying ahead in this legislative race has become increasingly essential.

12.1. Understanding the Challenges

Robotics poses unique ethical dilemmas that revolve around a central paradox: robots are inanimate objects, yet their programming and functioning can mimic independent thought and action. This raises questions of accountability, privacy, fairness, and autonomy, among others.

The first concern in this sphere is accountability. When a robot malfunctions or behaves inappropriately, who is responsible? Is it the programmer, the manufacturer, the end-user, or the robot itself? The law is still grappling with this conundrum, as it blurs the lines between product liability and individual liability.

Privacy is another key concern as robots, particularly those equipped with AI capabilities, collect and process vast amounts of data to function. In a world increasingly aware of the importance of data privacy and the potential misuse of personal information, how can we ensure robotic systems respect individual privacy rights?

Then, there's the question of fairness and bias. Systems that learn from their environments are potentially vulnerable to absorbing human prejudices, leading to biased decision-making.

Finally, there is the matter of autonomy. As robots increasingly take on human roles, the balance between robotic autonomy and human authority becomes more precarious, throwing up ethical and regulatory challenges.

12.2. Regulatory Models

Given the unique challenges presented by robotics, it's clear that traditional regulatory models may not suffice. Policymakers are increasingly considering alternative approaches to regulate this dynamic and complicated field.

Firstly, there is the concept of 'robot law' where legislation is tailored specifically to robotics. Typical laws governing objects and products may inefficiently cover robots that embody a degree of 'intelligence'.

Another possibility is the 'legal personhood' approach. This model, which is analogous to the way corporations are treated as individuals under the law, would potentially hold the robot itself responsible for its actions. However, this would require a sweeping redefinition of legal principles and stir up significant ethical controversy.

Regulatory sandboxes could also provide us with a solution. These controlled environments allow innovators to test their creations under a regulator's supervision before the robot enters into general use.

Finally, we have the 'ethics by design' approach, which ensures that ethical considerations are central to the design and programming of the robot.

12.3. Ethics in Robotics: Practical Applications

In efforts to address privacy concerns, robotic manufacturers could look into adopting privacy by design, a concept that involves building data protection systems directly into product design.

Eliminating bias in robotic decision-making can be challenging, particularly in algorithms that rely on machine learning. Here, the focus should be on transparent programming and ongoing monitoring to detect and correct bias.

Autonomy requires walking a tight rope between utility and control. Guided autonomy, where robots make decisions within prescribed boundaries, may offer a balanced solution.

These examples show it's feasible to tackle these novel ethical dilemmas, even if a one-size-fits-all solution seems elusive.

12.4. Final Thoughts

Developing ethical norms and regulatory frameworks for robotics is an ongoing process. However, one thing is clear, this dialogue needs to be inclusive. Scientists, policymakers, ethicists, and the public must be involved in shaping the rules that guide the future of robotics.

As the world contemplates the broader human rights, ethical, social, and legal implications of robotics, the legislation and design practices around robotics will remain a dynamic and evolving space. And perhaps therein lies the greatest excitement - that we are witnessing and participating in the birth of a new era, the era of robotics. It is an era that promises to redefine life as we know it, turning today's science fiction into tomorrow's reality.

www.ingramcontent.com/pod-product-compliance
Lightning Source LLC
Chambersburg PA
CBHW071032260726
48661CB00007B/3013